CALM EATING

DR RICK KAUSMAN

ALLEN&UNWIN

First published in 2001

Copyright © Dr Rick Kausman 2001

Quote credits: p.17, from *The Age*; p. 30, from *Breaking Free from Compulsive Eating*, Penguin Books, Melbourne; p.63, from *Overcoming Overeating*, Cedar, London; p.66 from *Australian Journal of Nutrition and Dietetics*, vol.2, 1995; p.70, from *Tuesdays with Morrie* by Mitch Albom, Doubleday; p.75, from *Real Gorgeous*, Allen & Unwin, Sydney; p.86, from *My First Love and Turning Points*, Julie Morgan, 1995; p.88, from *Big Kids*, New Harbinger Publications, Oakland; p. 97, from *Power Thought Cards*, 1991, Hay House Inc., California

Allen & Unwin
83 Alexander Street
Crows Nest NSW 2065
Australia
Phone: (61 2) 8425 0100
Fax: (61 2) 9906 2218
Email: info@allenandunwin.com
Web: www.allenandunwin.com

National Library of Australia
Cataloguing-in-Publication entry:

Kausman, Rick.
    Calm eating.

    ISBN 1 86508 726 2.

    1. Food habits. 2. Eating (Philosophy). I. Title.

641.013

Set in 12pt Goudy by Nada Backovic
Printed by McPherson's Priting Group, Maryborough, Vic

10 9 8 7 6 5 4 3 2 1

For many of us, managing our eating, weight and health has become a struggle. On the one hand, we would like to eat healthily so that we feel well and can enjoy a good quality of life. On the other hand, we're given so much information about what we *should* do to be healthy that it's easy to feel confused about how to approach this in the best way for us.

Just to complicate things even further, we've started to value food for what it doesn't have (fat and sugar, for example) rather than for the pleasure it brings us, and its sensory, social, symbolic, cultural and nutritional qualities. We have stopped *really* enjoying what can be a wonderful part of our lives—the food we eat.

Well, you *can* have your cake and eat it too. I hope *Calm Eating* goes some way to helping you quieten down concerns about how, what, when and how much to eat. I hope it helps you to not feel guilty, worried or anxious about eating foods that are a normal and pleasurable part of life. But above all, I hope it sets you on the path to the emotional and physical well-being that goes hand in hand with having an enjoyable relationship with food.

Dr Rick Kausman is a medical doctor who has worked in the area of eating behaviour and weight management for over fourteen years. His first book, *If Not Dieting, Then What?* (Allen & Unwin) was awarded Best Nutrition Writing, Australian Food Writers Award, 1999.

Rick is a committee member of Body Image and Health Inc., and has been an Executive Council member of the Australasian Society for the Study of Obesity since 1993. He is also a Fellow of the Australian College of Psychological Medicine and an Australian Medical Association (AMA) spokesperson on eating behaviour and weight management.

Rick is the creator of the healthy eating, healthy weight management website www.ifnotdieting.com. He is a regular speaker at both medical and corporate conferences, and is often interviewed by the print media, television and radio.

For further information, visit Dr Rick Kausman's website www.ifnotdieting.com or contact him at calmeating@ifnotdieting.com.au.

ALL FOOD IS MORALLY
NEUTRAL

Try to think of food as 'everyday' food
(rather than 'good' food) and 'sometimes' food
(rather than 'bad' or 'junk' food).

Enjoy food without feeling guilty.

If you feel guilty about eating, you usually eat more quickly, enjoy the food less and end up eating more. If you know it's okay to have it, it's much easier to eat more slowly, you usually enjoy your food more and you end up eating less!

It makes sense to accept food as a necessity and as a pleasure. It banishes deprivation, and brings back the ability to experience the physical and emotionally enjoyable offerings of food. It's not wrong to enjoy food.

SAMANTHA

4

A 'morally neutral' approach to food is imperative—being allowed to enjoy all sorts of food is an incredible relief. The guilt almost evaporates.

SALLY

5

If we know we can have it when we really
want it, and it's okay to have it if we really feel like it,
then we gain the power not to have it if we really don't
feel like it. If we think we aren't allowed to have it,
then we are made to want it all the more.

To my delight, I discovered that being free
to choose what and when to eat has given me the freedom
to choose to not eat.

ELEANOR

Desire is prompted by what we cannot have;
it is quenched when the veils are lifted.

ANONYMOUS

FEEDING YOUR SOUL

Try to eat slowly and enjoy your food.

The more we relax and enjoy our food,
the easier it is to get in touch with some of the natural
senses we have and were meant to use around food.

Fast food only tastes good when eaten fast;
if your taste buds dance slowly and sensually with it,
you realise it can't dance.

≈ ALAN ≈

Use as many of your senses as you can
to enjoy your food. Focus on the taste and texture,
the smell, how the food looks, and even how it
sounds when you eat it.

Now I had permission to relish it slowly. It was like coming out of a dark prison and seeing the sky for the first time in twenty years. Why did I do that to myself, ruin my enjoyment by rushing and gorging?

MARDIE

I am no longer a prisoner to food. I now take food and slowly have my evil way with it.

ALAN

It was a feeling of incredible freedom!
I could eat whatever I liked, and all I had to do for this
'amazing' privilege was to first sit down and carefully
think about what I really wanted.

MARDIE

A wonderful thing happened tonight.
I had one (count it, one) piece of chocolate after tea.
I ate it slowly and savoured every second of it sliding
around in my mouth. I ate one piece because I preferred
to have only one piece, just for the taste of it.
I was satisfied and content with that.

ELEANOR

15

Think about lunch and what you would like, enjoy that. Have that lunch and enjoy that. Think about that lunch later and enjoy it again. That makes for satisfaction.

ALAN

Food is seen in the modern context merely as something which feeds an engine ... leaded or unleaded. But we should remember, it also feeds the soul. It should be a sensuous pleasure, a repast enjoyed with family and friends, a source of pride and thanks in the offering of a bountiful table.

WENDY HARMER, from '*Good Weekend*'

The sense of self-satisfaction from creating your own food and especially sharing it with others is one of the greatest joys in life.

SHERRY CLEWLOW, from *If Not Dieting, Then What?*

INTUITIVE EATING

It can be scary to trust our intuition, but it is almost always dangerous not to trust it.

It is important to develop the balance between our nutritional knowledge and our natural instincts with regard to food. In other words, we need to get the balance right between using what we know and using how we feel.

Have faith in the human body—it is an amazing self-regulator. If we learn to listen rather than to dictate to our bodies, we can arrive at a far better understanding of ourselves as a whole.

SAMANTHA

22

If we aren't listening to what our bodies are saying, it becomes impossible for us to continue in the long term even if we are following the most beautifully balanced, nutritionally correct eating plan ever invented.

Very often, to get the balance right in the long term, we need to forget about the nutritional rules for a while and just concentrate on working out what our body wants.

To eat anything we really feel like and to instinctively know what it is without a fat/calorie counter screaming from the back of our heads is all a seasoned dieter needs to be free and happy.

SAMANTHA

EATING WITH
ALL YOUR SENSES

I can have it if I want it,
but do I really feel like it?

I can have it if I want it,
but will I really enjoy it?

We can all eat food when we are not really feeling physically hungry. It is quite normal to do some non-hungry eating (eating that we do when we are not physically hungry), but when we do too much it can tip our eating out of balance.

Sometimes it is difficult to tell the difference between a physical hunger and a feeling we get that makes us want to put food in our mouths.

It may be helpful to pause a few times during the course of a meal just to check out how you are going.

If we have been eating quickly and we are able to slow down, we are often able to pick up our own signals of fullness and satisfaction more easily.

... prolonging a meal does not stop it from ending. Sooner or later you have to get up from the table and go on to the next thing. And your choice is whether you go on to that next thing feeling comfortable and satisfied, or miserable and stuffed.

GENEEN ROTH,

from *Breaking Free From Compulsive Eating*

31

Many people assume that because it's breakfast, lunch or dinner-time, this means they must have something to eat.

Sometimes, eating is not really going to help the sort of feeling you have, so … sit down and try to work out what is making you feel that you want to eat.

It is helpful to know when we are eating for the taste of it, and when we are eating because of physical hunger. If we know we are eating something because it tastes great, we often need less food to feel satisfied than we would if we were eating because we were hungry. Understanding the difference can allow us to enjoy the food, feel satisfied, and not feel stuffed full afterwards.

With awareness and understanding
comes empowerment and choice.

If you are satisfied and not feeling like any more food, it is not a waste of food to put it away for another time, to throw it away, use it as compost, or to give it to the dog. It is a waste of food if you are still eating when you no longer feel like it.

Try not to get too hungry. Hunger signals are a bit like our bladder signals. If we wait too long to respond, we're more likely to have an accident!

If you eat any old thing when hungry instead
of what you desire, you will end up eating any old thing
and what you desire.

⪦ ALAN ⪧

DIETS DON'T WORK!

Dieting is like driving with your foot on the brake. Sooner or later, the tyres wear down and we skid out of control. If diets were faulty cars, we would be suing the manufacturer. Instead, we let them blame us.

DONNA

For many years, the word 'diet' has been used to mean 'a way of eating'. The meaning of the word has changed so much now that for most people it actually means the exact opposite—a way of not eating!

Dieting ... the deprivation and discipline,
it was like constantly holding my breath (and was
completely unmaintainable).

NICOLA

Most people use scales because they think the scales will help them control their weight—but very often the only thing the scales end up controlling is our thinking.

Research shows that after going on a diet, almost all the weight lost is regained. In fact, many people not only regain the weight they lose, but actually end up heavier than before they started the diet.

YOUR BODY

Health and vitality come in all shapes and sizes, and we can aim to be healthy at our own natural weight rather than thin at any cost.

Evidence shows that it is healthy behaviours, rather than the achievement of any particular weight, that determines optimal health.

By looking after ourselves and our bodies in the best way we can, our weight/size will evolve to the healthiest level that is possible.

Achieving and maintaining optimal well-being and, as a result of that, a healthy and comfortable weight, is very much like putting together the parts of a complex jigsaw puzzle. It is only by finding and working on the relevant issues for us, the relevant pieces of our puzzle, that the whole picture seems to fall into place.

There is no single magical goal

weight that any particular person is meant to be,
or stay at, all their adult life.

Being over our most comfortable weight is often a symptom of problems, rather than the cause. For me, seeing weight as a symptom has made it much easier to tackle. The fat is no longer the enemy. It becomes part of your body again, a part that is telling you that something isn't right. The reassociation with my physical self was very important. Like any armistice day, it was an incredible relief.

SAMANTHA

We can lead happy, healthy productive lives without being the current culture's idea of an ideal shape.

I am no longer putting off my life until
I reach some magic weight.

HELEN

NATURAL EATING

There is no one way of eating that is right
for everyone all the time. There is no final arriving,
rather a continual learning.

THEA O'CONNOR, from *If Not Dieting, Then What?*

Normal or natural eating is many things to many people. Not only is there variety from person to person, there is also enormous variety within each individual.

It is normal or natural to eat more on some days and less on other days.

It is normal or natural to eat certain types of foods some of the time, just for the taste of it.

It is normal or natural to overeat occasionally.

It is normal or natural to undereat occasionally.

Remember, no single meal makes any significant difference in the long term.

It is normal or natural for women to have fluctuations in appetite and in cravings for certain types of food as hormone levels vary during the course of the menstrual cycle.

It is normal or natural to eat less of the foods you enjoy the taste of now, because it's okay to have them again another time.

TRUE BEAUTY

It's important to note that changing our body doesn't necessarily lead to a better body image or a better self-esteem.

Try shifting your focus from what you look like, to being comfortable in your body.

Acceptance does not imply self-delusion. It involves coming to terms with what is. When you accept yourself you simply say, 'This is how I am right now. I don't know what the future will bring. I do know that if I want to change, I must first feel as comfortable as I can with myself in the present.'

HIRSCHMANN and MUNTER, from
Overcoming Overeating

By accepting and understanding who you are—your power, your vulnerability, your strength and your imperfections—you can make changes.

If you are an adult woman, it really is all
right to look like an adult woman.

PENELOPE GOWARD, from *If Not Dieting, Then What?*

Even I don't look like Cindy Crawford
when I get up in the morning.

CINDY CRAWFORD

The models of Rubens, Rembrandt, Gaugin and Matisse were all rounded, plump women. Some art critics believe that the supreme of female beauties from the Renaissance, Leonardo Da Vinci's Mona Lisa, may have been pregnant at the time, inferring that female roundness and heaviness were considered most beautiful.

JENNIFER O'DEA, from 'Body Image...
A Review of the Literature'

Irrespective of where a person falls in the
continuum of weight, they deserve to be respected and
supported in obtaining self-acceptance.

FIONA MCDONALD, from *If Not Dieting, Then What?*

Be with people who respect and
accept you for yourself. Be discerning about the amount
of time you spend with people who are always focused
on looks and food.

Recognise negative self-talk about your body, speak
gently to yourself, and try to do some rephrasing
of this self-talk.

Work on some positive affirmations
about your body.

The culture we have does not make people feel good about themselves. And you have to be strong enough to say if the culture doesn't work, don't buy it.

MORRIE SCHWARTZ, from *Tuesdays with Morrie*

Protect yourself from cultural bombardment.

Before industrialisation, clothes were made to fit an individual. Mass production then led to standardisation of clothing shapes and sizes. Instead of the clothes fitting the body, the emphasis shifted to the body fitting the clothes.

From my experience, clearing out my wardrobe of all my too-small clothes was one of the most liberating things I could have done, and taking care to make sure that I had something comfortable to wear was also nurturing.

BEV

Have been a bit kinder to myself in
terms of body image ... grappling with the concept that I
am much more than what size I am. Even daringly
wearing some clothes to work that I wouldn't normally
wear. It would not be true to say that I want to stay this
size forever, but I am nevertheless trying to focus on the
good points rather than the ones I don't like so much.

JOANNE

It is possible to lead a happy and fulfilling life without having the so-called ideal body shape.

It's important to accept our inherited physical characteristics.

You are not your buttocks.

KAZ COOKE, from *Real Gorgeous*

NURTURING
YOUR TRUE SELF

Sometimes, people feel they are being selfish if they think about their own needs. But being selfish is very different from being self-caring. Being selfish is looking after one's own needs to the exclusion of others. Being self-caring is understanding that you, too, have important needs that must be met; that you are worthy, and that you have a responsibility to yourself.

Give yourself the right to say 'no'.

Accept that you only have a finite emotional space.

If we look after our own needs, we feel more
energised, in control and positive. We are then much
more likely to look after ourselves in an appropriate way,
and to enjoy caring for and giving to others.

We all need and like to feel
looked after and appreciated.

I'm good enough just as I am.

How about I say to myself it's okay not
to be perfect at this. I can roll with this and make it
up as I go along. I don't have to have some huge game
plan, strategy thing with lots of rules. I can just take it
a day at a time, a meal at a time. And I can change what
I'm doing any time I like. Just give myself permission to
do what feels right at the time, not what I
should be doing or have to do …

NICOLA

If you think you are too small to be effective you've
never been in bed with a mosquito!

ANITA RODDICK, founder of *The Body Shop*

TAKING FLIGHT

For many of us, being fit for living is a much more appropriate outcome of increasing our physical activity than being fit to run a marathon.

Without actually shivering with ecstasy when the mind bows down in homage before beauty, it is possible, while walking, to cross the boundaries of the mind and the heart. There is serene joy in the knowledge that thought can enter completely into feeling and feeling can enter completely into thought.

ELIZABETH JOLLEY, from *My First Love* and *Turning Points*

Whatever physical activity we
can do is worthwhile.

Physical activity is vital in allowing us to achieve
and maintain optimal health and quality of life.

The notion of 'no pain, no gain' should
be equated with 'no brain'.

GREGORY ARCHER, from *Big Kids*

I went for a short walk and thought …
I can go as far or as short as I like. In fact, I enjoy
walking, slowly watching the trees and the houses,
breathing fresh air. It doesn't have to be a drag,
a pain, an exercise that one must do to gain 'good girl'
points in life. I am doing this for me!

⁓ MARDIE ⁓

It was lack of exercise, lack of worrying about myself, looking after the kids and never eating properly. One day I found myself walking along the foreshore taking in the scenery and all of a sudden I thought—where am I? I realised I had gone for miles, and I thought this is wonderful, now I can walk again.

MARYANNE

If you don't like a certain type of physical
activity, don't keep doing it—try something else.
Be prepared to try things. You aren't failing if you try
something and realise it isn't for you.

ONE DAY AT A TIME

Small changes can make a big difference.

Going off focus is normal in
the process of change.

Off focus times can be used as a
learning opportunity.

Progress is succeeding at
small steps along the way.

If we want to make long-term changes,
we can only continue to work on what we can change
in a long-term way.

... it takes some time from the first declaration
to the final demonstration. So be patient.

LOUISE L. HAY, from *Power Thought Cards*

ACKNOWLEDGMENTS

This book would not have been possible without the many clients who have shared their experiences and helped me to understand the important issues in this complex area of health. I would particularly like to thank the clients who took the time and emotional energy to share their own feelings in stories or quotes, some of which are featured in this book.

I would like to thank Pen Goward for her inspirational work in the 1980s and the early 1990s, and the many health professionals with whom I have regular contact and who provide wonderful support and encouragement.

I would also like to thank the following people for their help: Sue Reynolds, for giving me the push to really get this book off the ground; Eva Friedman, for her readiness to lend a hand and for her way with words; Annette Barlow, my publisher at Allen &Unwin, whose support has been never ending; Karen Penning, my editor, and Nada Backovic, my designer, who have both done a great job presenting the information and ideas I handed to them in a most easy to use and appealing way; my daughters, Elise and Meaghan, who continue to be my pride and joy; and my wife, Nikki, for her unconditional love and support.

Printed in Great Britain
by Amazon